9.95

SAND
AND OTHER POEMS

SAND
AND OTHER POEMS

MAHMOUD DARWEESH

Selected and translated from the Arabic by
RANA KABBANI

KPI

LONDON, NEW YORK, SYDNEY AND HENLEY

First published in 1986 by KPI Limited
14 Leicester Square, London WC2H 7PH, England

Distributed by
Routledge & Kegan Paul plc
14 Leicester Square, London WC2H 7PH, England

Routledge & Kegan Paul Inc
29 West 35th Street
New York, NY 10001, USA

Routledge & Kegan Paul
Methuen Law Book Company
44 Waterloo Road
North Ryde, NSW 2113
Australia

Routledge & Kegan Paul plc
Broadway House, Newtown Road
Henley-on-Thames
Oxon RG9 1EN, England

Set in 10/13 Sabon
and printed in Great Britain
by Butler & Tanner Ltd
Frome, Somerset

this translation © Rana Kabbani 1986

No part of this book may be reproduced in any form
without permission from the publisher, except for the
quotation of brief passages in criticism

ISBN 07013-0062-X

Mahmoud Darweesh was born in Palestine in 1942. As a child of six, he recalls how his native village of Al-Birwa was destroyed by the Israeli army. A refugee in his own country, he moved to the Galilee where he began writing. He worked as a journalist in Haifa, but as his poetry became more popular, he became a victim of Israeli military harassment. He was jailed many times, and finally put under house arrest.

In 1970, Darweesh was forced to leave his country, and resided in Beirut where he edited *Shu'un Filastiniyya*. In 1982, after the Israeli invasion of Lebanon, he was forced out again, and now lives in exile in Europe, where he edits the literary periodical *Al-Karmel*. He is considered the most influential poet writing in Arabic today. He has published eleven volumes of poetry and three of prose. He is the winner of the Lotus Prize, 1969, the Mediterranean Prize, 1980, and the Lenin Prize, 1982.

Contents

1 If I could choose again from the beginning   1
2 We walk towards a land   3
3 Earth narrows before us   5
4 The flute speaks   7
5 Sand   9
6 Al-Mutanabbi's voyage into Egypt   11
7 Gypsy song   17
8 Sirhan drinks his coffee in the cafeteria   19
9 The river is the stranger   25
10 Always   29
11 The train at One   31
12 I asked you to take me as autumn and river   33
13 On Fifth Avenue he greeted me   35
14 Words   41
15 I love the seas I love   43
16 Birds die in Galilee   45
17 Woman   47
18 Beirut   49
19 Fog on a mirror   59
20 Last evening in Paris   61
21 Another year only   67
22 Pigeons settle, pigeons fly   73
   Index of first lines   79

If I could choose again from the beginning

If I could choose again from the beginning
I would still choose the things that I have chosen,
The roses curling on the same brown fences,
The paths that may or may not lead me to Cordoba

Again I'd link my shadow to the dry rocks
That homeless birds might make their small nests there.
I'd break my shadow for a scent of almonds
Descended from a cloud.
Come near to me and listen,
Come share this bread and wine.
I love those lands untainted by departure,
I love those women hiding passions
Like the death of stallions
In their hearts.
I would return once more,
Could I return,
To my same rose
To my same steps
But never to Cordoba.

We walk towards a land

We walk towards a land not of our flesh,
Not of our bones its chestnut trees,
Its stones unlike the curly goats
Of the Song of Songs.
We walk towards a land
That does not hang a special sun for us.
Mythic women clap:
A sea around us,
A sea upon us.
If wheat and water do not reach you,
Eat our love and drink our tears.
Black veils of mourning for the poets.
You have your victories and we have ours,
We have a country where we see
Only the invisible.

Earth narrows before us

Earth narrows before us,
Traps us in the final passage.
We pull our limbs off
So that we might pass through,
If only we could be earth's wheat
That we might die to live.
If only we could be earth's children
That she might pity us.

Where can we go on crossing this last border?
Where do birds fly after the final sky?
Where do plants sleep when all the winds have passed?
We write our names in coloured smoke
And we die in this final passage
That olive trees might grow
To mark our place.

The flute speaks

The flute speaks.
If I could only pass
Into Damascus like the echo.

Silk sleeps at her shore,
Curves in cries
That die before I reach them
Distance falls
Like tears.

The flute calls.
It turns the sky
Into a woman and a woman
It parts a road
To make us part.

Did I suffer all in vain,
Did I break the mountain rocks
And love's first apple.
A sword of distance calls
Damascus
My woman
I want to love and stay.

If I could only pass
Into Damascus like the echo.
Flute,
Be yet more gentle with me.
If I could speak your tears
I would possess Damascus.

Sand

Endless place of thought,
And woman,
Shall we seek you to the grave?

Trees, at first, were female,
Made from words and water.
Does earth die like man,
Does the bird carry it
To seed a secret space?

I am the beginning and the end.

Sand
A shape and an idea of shape
Sand
Oblivion killing blossom
Everything miraculous
Sand
A country made of sand
I lost my woman and my mind
In sand.

Shape of every tree to come,
Clouds that look like houses,
One colour merely for all oceans
And for sleep.
I see kingdoms of sand,
And yet I'm torn apart by torrents
Like a foolish bird.
I think the arrow is my rib,
As I choke on sand.
I lost my words, my woman
In the sand.

Two lovers find their way
Despite this sand.
They find a secret river
And they say to one another
How brief this stretch of sand.

Sand.
I am the beginning and the end.

Al-Mutanabbi's Voyage into Egypt

The Nile has its habits
And I am leaving.

I pass quickly through these lands
Which steal my names from me.
I've come from Aleppo
But will not go back to Baghdad.
The North has fallen
And I've found no path
To lead me to myself
Or Egypt.

I heard the distant neighing
But saw neither horse nor horseman
Each voyage leads me to another
I've found no country here
I've found no countrymen.

The earth is slimmer
Than the passing of a sword
Through a narrow waist.
The earth is wider.
Than a prophet's tent.
I see no one behind me,
I see no one before me.
I feel a solitude in crowds.

My country is my latest poem.

When I walk toward myself
The villages expel me
I break mirrors and I shatter.
I see nations being handed out
Like tokens,
I see slaves in slavish wars
Eating other slaves.
I see the bend in every bend.
My country is my latest poem.
The night is mine, and longing.
And yet no ebony lover
Tears me into shreds,
No cluster of frail trees
Lures me into sleep
Beside this Nile.
When I walk toward myself
The villages expel me.

Egypt is not in Egypt.
I find only emptiness
When I seek her there.
The Nile has its habits,
And I am leaving.

Stone am I.
Egypt,
Will my regret reach you
In this dry year?

My steps are my ideas
My blood my dust.

You left the river open
To each comer
Who descends from boats
To your thighs of throne and ivory.
Did the throne exist before the water?

They ascend the pyramids to rape.
I am inert and empty-handed,
That I know,
But every time I try to weep for you
You leave me for my foe.
You left the river open
For me to fling myself
Into the Nile.

The pagan priest shall not abduct
My daughters
Nor shall he weave a banner
From our shrouds.

You go barefoot to pick cotton
In the South.
The silence banishes the difference
Between the soil and peasants.
Have the poets all left Egypt?

God's land is narrow,
And narrower still
This carpet of red sand.
The tomb is Egypt's master
Egypt sleeps in the shadow
Of the tomb.

Every time I say I will forget her
She pursues my soul
And makes the whole of Syria alienation.
She makes each woman that I touch
A memory,
She makes my footsteps paths
Or alphabets of departure to the poem
Of flame.
I will not return to Aleppo
For having left
I've lost the road that leads back
To Aleppo.
The Nile has its habits
And I am leaving.

Each man who seeks you
Is stolen by departure.
The Romans are spread out
Across our alphabet,
The poor are crying
Beneath our alphabet.
I am the fortress and the siege,
I am the similarity of names
Upon the royal ladder.

What has happened to this Nile?
It has not taken my tears with it
In its sudden downpour,
It has not poured me sudden spring
Or imperious anger.
Egypt's silence breaks me
Here is her slave prince
Here are her hungry.
I sell the palace a song
I break the palace
With a song
I lean against the wind and wound
And am not sold.

The Romans spread out across our alphabet.
No sword disperses them
All swords diminish me
Give me back my names
I am the killer killed
Give me back my names.

Gypsy song

A clear street
And a girl
Who comes out to light the moon.
My land is far,
A land without a trace.

A salty dream
And a voice
That carves a shape in stone.
Move, my love,
Across my lashes or these chords.

A cruel moon
And a calm
That breaks the wind and rain
That makes the river a needle
In hands that embroider leaves.

A savage time
And death
That takes us as it goes.
We have approached the river
We have ended the voyage.

A clear street
And a girl
Who comes out to paste up pictures
On my corpse.
My tents are far away,
Tents without a trace.

Sirhan drinks his coffee in the cafeteria

They arrive.
Our doors are the sea.
The rain surprised us.
No God but God.
The rain surprised us, and the bullets.
The earth here is a carpet,
And they continue to arrive.

You do not know the day.
You cannot tell the colour,
Nor the taste. Nor the voice.
You do not know the shape.
Sirhan is born, and Sirhan grows.
He drinks the wine and raves,
He draws his killer and he tears the picture,
He kills him when he sees his final shape.

Sirhan writes upon his jacket's sleeve
And memory takes a bird's beak
And eats the wheat of Galilee.

What was love?
Hands that were expressive,
Chains and prisons being formed,
Exiles being born.
We wrap around your name.
We were a people now we are of stone.
You were a country now you are of smoke.
Old chains are bracelets of blown roses
Old chains are maidenhead and passion
In this new exile.

Sirhan lies when he says he drank your milk.
Sirhan grew up in the kitchens of a ship
Which never touched your shores.

>What is your name?
>I've forgotten.
>What is your father's name?
>I've forgotten.
>And your mother's?
>I've forgotten.
>Did you sleep last night?
>I slept for an eternity.
>Did you dream?
>I dreamt.

He cried suddenly:
>Why did you drink the oil you smuggled
>From the wounds of Christ?

We saw his fingers begging.
We saw him measuring the sky with chains.
Lands that change their people,
Stars that spread like pebbles.
He sang:
Our generation passed and died.
The killers bred in us the victims grew in us
Blood like water.
Mothers who married enemies.
We called out, 'wheat!'
The echo came back 'war'
We called out, 'home!'
The echo came back 'war'
We called out, 'Jaffa!'
The echo came back 'war'
From that day on we measured skies with chains.

Sirhan laughs in the kitchens of the ship.
He holds a tourist and is lost.
All lands are far that lead to Nazareth.
All lands are far except for Nazareth.

Songs speak to him, and holidays make him lonely.
The smell of coffee is geography.
They exiled you.
They murdered you.
Your father hid behind the texts
And watched them come.
The smell of coffee is a tender hand.
The smell of coffee is a voice that takes you.
The smell of coffee is a sound that gurgles
Like the water in the alleys when it rains.

Sirhan knows more than one language
Or one woman. He has a pass to leave the ocean
He has another pass to enter it.
He is a drop of blood looking for its wound.
The smell of coffee is geography.
He drinks his coffee and he dreams.

You were born here. Yet you live there.
Your city does not sleep. It has no lasting names.
Houses change inhabitants,
Windows leave their places as they enter memory.
Sirhan draws a shape then cancels it.
He does not read the papers, so how does sorrow
Reach him?

What is Jerusalem but a stance for speeches,
But a step to hungry power?
What is Jerusalem but cigarettes and liquor?
Yet it is my country.
You would not find a difference
Between its curved fields
And my palm.
You could not find the difference
Between the night that sleeps in memory
And the night upon the Carmel.

He tears the clouds apart
And throws them at the winds.

I ate. I drank. I slept. I dreamt.
I learnt a vowel.
He writes: ظ ع ط ض ص
And they disappear before him,
The dins of oceans in them,
The din of silence in them.
Letters to distinguish us from others.
We stone them with our diphthongs.
Shall we fight?
What matter,
Since the Arab revolution
Remains preserved in anthems,
In flags and at the bank.
In your wounds' name they speak their speech.
Christ becomes a dealer
Who signs away his merchandise of cloth.
No sky for you except this tent:
It burns, you burn.

We come to you as prisoners or corpses.
Sirhan a prisoner of the peace and war.
He reads the details of his fate
On the wall behind the stripper's legs:
Your war is two wars,
Your war is two wars.

Sirhan!
Did you kill?
Sirhan is silent.
He drinks his coffee and he dreams.
He draws a map without a border in it.
He measures earth with chains.
He draws a picture of his killer,
He rips it up,
Then kills it when it takes a final shape.

The river is the stranger

The river is the stranger
She said
And she went to meet her singing.
We did not try love's language,
Nor seek the river in vain,
But night rose from her garments
A night like no night I had known.
I made an offering in its name
That saints might die in place of us
An offering of my blood
In order to remain
A little longer on these steps,
A little longer in her singing.

Alone in the small aloneness
Flowers on the water
Feet upon the water
Where shall we go,
Being wound and knife,
My small bird of exile,
Where shall we go?

Sometimes a poet might chance an hour
Higher than the water's level,
Lower than the gallows.
How can I bid you leave,
When you are the moment of meeting
Between farewells?

If I say that love comes
As death comes
When we do not await love
I say don't wait for me.

The river is the stranger
She said
As she went to meet the road.
The wide streets all know nothing about Jhana
Except that raindrops do not touch her,
Except that it was I who changed,
Became enmeshed in lightning and in trees.
Did the land I clung to,
Did the earth I lived in become journey?

Alone we cannot enter night.
Why does your body long for lotus blossom
Growing further than my grave?

Reshape me into moon,
That I might slant the night
Behind me into forests.
Reshape me into stone,
That I might draw the distance to me,
As horses follow shyly.

This earth has taught me craters
That are absent from your eyes
So do not wait for me.

The river is the stranger
She said
As she went to meet her tears.
She was not lovelier than the cafe waitress,
Nor nearer than my mother,
But night became a kitten in her lap,
And the wide horizon
Slipped in through the shutter
Just to seek a shelter in her gaze.

Go become the dream, Jhana.
Jhana wept,
And I was thrown into an hour
Where all dreams were shards of broken glass.

Jhana
You could not be the cities I was seeking
Nor the land that I desired
That I might stop the river's taking me in embrace.
Why do you seek me now,
As if you were the river or the lover in the river,
Why do you leave me now,
When for you I still must linger on this earth.
Jhana wept,
And the river gave me ribbons to enwrap me
As the sky forgot its shape.

Always

At night
We hear approaching footsteps
And the door escapes our room
As if it were a cloud migrating.

Your blue shadow
Who steals it nightly
From my bed?
Your eyes are regions
Where I've never been.
Be trees
That I might see your shadow
Be moons
That I might see your shadow
Be glass
That I might see your shadow
In my shadow
Petals upon ash.

The train at One

A man and a woman parting,
Flinging roses off their hearts
Breaking
Shadow leaving shadow
Turning into three
A man and a woman and the street.

The train does not arrive
So they return to the cafe
They say some different words
They watch the dawn emerge
From the strings of a guitar.

I look into the regions of my heart
Friends and towns have called me
To forgetfulness in the cellars of Madrid.
I forget nothing of a woman
But my rapture and her face.
I forget you I forget you I forget

If we had been a little late
For the train at One
If we had sat another hour
In the Greek cafe
If returning birds had passed us
If we had read the evening papers
We would have been
A man and a woman
Meeting.

I asked you to take me as autumn and river

I asked you to take me as autumn and river,
I asked you to cross the stream without me
And fill the fields together.
I asked you to take me as autumn,
To wilt in you and rise together.
I asked you to take me as river,
To be my memory
In this winter.

All things unite us that divide us.
All things renew us that disperse us.
How can you be my life's amazement
When
I know that women are unfaithful to all lovers
Except mirrors.
I know that earth forgets all lovers but the dead.

You are asleep when the high waves steal me –
At your breast's edge the sea begins.
Two strangers.
Your hair, my roof.
Your palms, my voice.
Your love, my sword.
Your eyes, two rivers.
Your presence, my dying.
Your absence, my death.

On Fifth Avenue he greeted me
(For Rashid Hussein)

On Fifth Avenue he greeted me.
He leaned against a wall of glass.
There are no willows in New York.
He brought tears to my eyes,
He gave the river back its waters,
We drank coffee,
And parted seconds after.

For twenty years
I've known him to be forty
Tall as a coastal song
He came to us a blade of wine
And left, a prayer's end.
He flung out poems
At Christo's Restaurant
And all of Acre would rise from sleep
To walk upon the sea.

He had roses. He had chains.
Nothing hurt him behind barbed wires
But his mighty wound.
Lovers would pass and promise meetings,
There were seacoasts that we lifted,
There were wild grapes that we tasted,
There were blue herbs that cried out
And we mingled in their cry.

We tore all songs apart,
We were torn apart by gazes
From dark eyes.
We fought and we were killed.
While the knights came and went.

In every void
We saw the singer's silence
Blue to the point of vanishing.
For twenty years
He has been throwing his flesh
In all directions
To the fowl and fish.

The son of two peasants
From a limb of Palestine,
Southern and pious,
He was big of feet
And pale of voice.
Brown to the point of familiarity,
He was poor as any butterfly.

He could see further
Than prison gates
He could see closer
Than studies on Art
He could see us,
See our refugee cards.

Simple, in cafes and in language
He liked the flute, and beer
The prose of meadows
The poetry of wheat.

He visited his family Saturdays
To rest from the terrible, divine ink
And the police's questioning.
He only published
Two slim books of his early poems
And gave us all the rest.

... Pale as the sun in New York,
From where will the heart pass,
Is there room, in this asphalt wood,
For the feathers of a dove?
My mailbox is empty
And dawn here does not sting
Nor any star burn in this crowding.

My evenings are narrow.
The body of my love is paper
No one wraps around my evenings,
Wishing to be river and cloud.
From where will the heart pass,
Who will pick up the dream
Fallen outside the bank and opera house?
A cascade of pins
Drowns my ancient desires.

I no longer dream
I desire to desire
No. This is not my time.
Give me my limbs to embrace
And my winds to go forth.

From cafe to cafe
I want the other language
I want the difference
Between fire and memory.
Give me my limbs to embrace
And my winds to go forth.

Why do poems evade me when I'm far from Jaffa?
Why does Jaffa vanish when I touch her with my hand?
No, this is not my time.

He disappeared down Fifth Avenue
Or a Northern Pole
And all I remember of his eyes
Were cities that come and go.
He vanished.

We met again in a year
At the airport in Cairo
He said
If only I were free
In the prison cells of Nazareth.

He slept a week.
He woke two days.
He drank nothing of the coffee
But its colour.

We retraced our past steps,
The land that crawls in our blood like insects,
The death of friends,
Those who shared our days,
Then scattered.
They did not love us as we wished them to.
They did not love us, but they knew us.

He would rave when he woke
And wake when he wept.
Life has passed me by
And I've lost the essence of it all.
He disappeared with a sunset
Over the deep Nile
And I prepared a eulogy for him,
A funeral of palm.

My continuous suicide,
Can't we start again from any parting,
Can't you glow like the plants of Galilee
Or flame like a murdered man?
He disappeared.

On Fifth Avenue he greeted me.
He leaned against a fountain of cement.
There are no willows in New York.
Has anyone of us died? No.
Have you changed? No.
Is the journey still the journey
With the harbour in the heart?

He was so far
That he vanished like a deer
In a lake of fog.

He did not know or ask the time
Nor was he moved by those upright trees
Beneath his tenth floor window
In Manhattan
He only listened to the secret ringing
Of his bell
And saw another winter come.

Are we to remain like this,
Moving to the outside
In this orange day
Only to touch
The dark and vague inside?

I carry the earth's weight
Girls have taken of my soul and gone.
Birds have nested in my voice,
Then have broken me and flown.
And the singing has dispersed me,
And misplaced me.

No, this is not my time.
No, this is not my flesh.

Words

When my words were wheat
I was earth.
When my words were anger
I was storm.
When my words were rock
I was river
When my words turned honey
Flies covered my lips.

I love the seas I love

I love the seas I love
I love the lands I love
And yet
One drop of water
On the feathers
Of a bird
In Haifa
Can wash me
Of the sins
I will commit.

Birds die in Galilee

We will meet in a while,
In a year,
In two years,
In sixteen.
She threw into her camera
Twenty gardens
And the birds of Galilee.

She could not know that we gave her,
Death and I, the secrets of love
At the custom's gate.
So she must leave what makes wheat
The lashes of the earth,
What makes volcanoes
Another name for jasmine.

Nothing tired me at night
Except her silence
When it spread out like a street.
Be what you must, Rita,
Make the silence an axe
Or a frame for stars
Or a place for a tree in labour.

Flocks of birds fell like paper
Into the wells
And when I lifted the blue wings
I saw a growing grave.
I am the man on whose skin
Chains have carved a country.

Woman

Woman who holds the Mediterranean
In her lap
You are the only cry
The only space for silence.

My skin and voice have joined.
Beneath my windows
Winds pass that carry guards,
And the dark arrives
Without appointment.
I see you and my stature then.
You are the only singing
You sing me when I'm silent
You are the only silence.

Beirut

Butterfly of stone
The spirit's shape when mirrored
The testament of earth in the feathers of a dove,
Beirut of tiredness and gem
The wheat stalk's death,
The wandering of a star
Between me and my woman.
I had not heard my blood speak
In a lover's name before
As it spoke and slept Beirut.

From the slight seaward rain
We found our names,
And from the taste of Fall.
From the shape of oranges
Coming from the south
As if we were our fathers
Arriving at Beirut
In order to arrive.
From the slight rain we built our huts
In the high grass we dug our holes like ants
And slept in hope of Beirut that was tent and star.

Enslaved we were in the spineless times.
Our captors threw us at our families,
When we fell our guardians sang
And spoke the words:
From a king on the throne
To a king in the tomb.

Enslaved we were in the spineless times.
We could not find a final likeness
But our blood.
We could not tell what made the monarch popular,
Or the guard less fierce.
We could not find a thing to show our own identity
Except our blood in stains upon the wall.
We softly sang
Beirut our tent
Beirut our star.

A window giving on the leaden sea.
A curving street that charmed us,
Or an ancient tune.
More lovely than the poems of it
And simpler than speech.
Endless shapes of cities
And new alphabets
Beirut our only tent
Beirut our only star.

We stretched ourselves upon her willows
To measure bodies that the sea had rubbed away.
We came to Beirut from our childhood names
To search for southern space,
For a vessel to contain the heart.
The heart melted, it melted.
We stretched ourselves upon the ruins
To weigh the north with the weight of chains.
The shadows wilted,
They broke and they dispersed us,
The shadows lengthened to embrace a tree

We were the cluster of dead bodies
Hanging from its branches.
We came from land denied us,
We came from pompous language
And from weariness.
This desolation stretches
From the ruler's palace
To our prison cells,
From our first dreams
To ash.
So give us just one wall
From which to call, 'Beirut!'
On which to hang these many kingdoms
Selling oil and humans.
Give us one small wall
On which to stand and cry:
Beirut our final tent,
Beirut our final star.

A leaden space scattered all through space.
From the Gulf to Hell,
From Hell to the Gulf,
From right to the right
To the moderate middle
A hanging-tree for millions.

Beirut
Where are the arcades of Cordoba?
I cannot be exiled more than once
Nor can I love you more than once
I do not see in ocean
Anything but ocean.

Beirut
Witness of the heart
I leave her streets and leave myself
Clutched by an endless poem.
My fire won't die down,
The doves are on the rooftops
Peace upon the remnants of the rooftops.
I fold the city as I fold my papers
And carry it away, a sack of clouds.
I wake and look in my body's clothing
For myself.
We laugh and say that we are still alive.
I open up the narrow street for wind
For footsteps
For the crafty seller of hot bread.
Grace of Beirut as she stands in fog,
Gratitude to Beirut as she stands in ruin.
The conquerors have led me to the poem
I carry language docile as a cloud
Above the pavement
Of reading and of writing
This sea has left its eyes with us
And gone back towards sea.

From a stone they built their ghetto nation
From a stone we'll build a lover's country
From a stone
I voice my slow farewell
The city drowns in repetitious phrases
The wound grows on the sword
And both come near to cut me.

I descend the stairs
That do not end in cellars of festivity
I descend the stairs
That do not end in poems.
For longing's sake I head towards Damascus
Perhaps I'll have a vision
Perhaps the ringing bells will echo
Till they make me shy.
Words were consequential
When they changed the one who spoke them.
Farewell to all that's yet to come
To dawn about to break and break us
To cities returning us to other cities
To curved swords and palm.
Our journey lengthens with our wound.

I see a dove fly from one heart burnt by the past
To another heart to a rooftop of brown brick.
Did the fighter pass this way,
Did the falling shrapnel break the cafe plates?
I see nations cardboard-strong with kings and khaki.
I see cities crowning their new conquerors.

The East is opposite to the West sometimes,
And the West's East too
Its image and its chattel.
I see cities crowning their new conquerors,
I see rulers who will export martyrs
So as to import beer
And the latest instruments
Of torture and of sex.

I see cities hang their lovers
From steel trees.
What are we leaving but this jail?
What do prisoners ever have to leave?
We walk towards a distant song
Or freedom
We touch earth's beauty
For the first time in our lives
This is a blue dawn,
The wind can be touched and tasted
Like a fig.

We ascend
One,
Three,
A hundred and a thousand,
In the name of sleeping people
At this hour
At dawn at dawn we finish our first poem
We tidy up the chaos
And we bless the life
We bless the ones
Who are alive.

Moon above Baalbek
Blood upon Beirut
From a form without a meaning
To a meaning with no form
Was Beirut a mirror we could break
To enter through its fragments
Or were we mirrors broken by the breeze?

Did the Church change
When the priest put on his khaki
Or was it the victim who had changed,
Did the Church change
Or was it we who changed?

Streets encircle us
As we walk among the bombs
    Are you used to death?
    I'm used to life and to endless desire.
    Do you know the dead?
    I know the ones in love.
A bullet flies above us
As we follow details of the war.
Did we form our poems in vain
Or did the war root out the poem?
We seek rhythm in a stone
But cannot find it
The poets have their ancient gods.
A bomb explodes
So we enter this hotel to drink.
    I like Rimbaud's silence
    His letters which speak Africa.
    I've lost Cavafy, for he warned me
    Not to leave Alexandria.
    I found Kafka sleeping just beneath my skin.
    A cloak of desolation
    The police inside us.
    What do you see on that horizon?
    Another far horizon and another.

Besieged we were
By the sea and Holy Books.
Are we finished?
No.
We will survive like ancient ruins do,
Like a skull we will keep shape.

Saturday. Thursday. Language. Chaos.
The jeweller's shop,
Police interrogation.
Tuesday evening.
They climbed the steps and looted.
They strummed their strings
And sang
When they smelled our burning flesh.

We burned our boats.
We hung our planets from barbed wires.
We were not seeking ancestry
In the scratches on the map.
We did not stray
From the purity of bread
Or from our mud-stained shirts.
We were not born to ask
How life came forth from matter.
We were born, and slept on straw,
And drew the wagons like exhausted horses.
Then we burned our boats and hugged our guns.

Do you know the dead?
I know the ones unborn.
They will be born beneath the trees,
They will be born under the rain,
They will be born from stone,
They will be born from broken glass,
They will be born in corners,
From defeats, from mirrors,
They will be born from shrapnel,
From bracelets, from blossoms,
From stories.
They will be born and they will grow,
They will be born and killed,
They will be born and born and born.

Beirut
Markets on the sea,
A nation in a rented flat,
Cafes turning to the sun like sunflower.
Paradise of minutes,
Mountains bowing to the sea.
Beirut
Streets that end in ships
A seaport where the cities gather
Architecture for the newly-moneyed leisure
Fossils of our days turned up by the tide
A world that's coming to new markets
Rising like the dollar,
Like the price of gold
That follow in their rising
The streams of eastern blood.

And we will wake this earth
Which leaned against our blood
We will draw our dead ones
From its secret cells
To wash their bodies with our whitest tears,
To pour the spirit's milk for them to drink,
To sprinkle words upon their fragile lids:
Wake up wake up and walk back with us to our homes
Come listen to the wind among the roofs,
The wind that wrenched the southern prairies
From our arms
You are the land we guard
Whose curves and wheat we love
The only land we have to stand upon
Come back come back to us once more
We will not leave the region of your blood
And we will keep you from oblivion
The sun has scorched us
Your sharp bones make us bleed
But still we call to you
The echo comes back homeland
From our blood to our blood
Are the limits of the earth.

Beirut
A dream that we shall carry where we will.
A wooden lily and the first embrace.
A poem of stone
A flower spoken is Beirut,
A child that broke the mirrors
And then slept.

Fog on a mirror

We know place
We've followed after all our dead
But can no longer hear them.
We've moved aside the times,
We've moved aside the first night.

In the siege of blood and sun we wait
With defeated language.
My mother calls me.
I cannot see her for the dust.

We know words
We know the brandished mottoes:
Our sun is mightier than your night
Our martyrs rise again
They rise again as fruit,
As flags,
And flowing streams.
They arrive.
They arrive.
They arrive.

{ ON – lesung }
{ + Bilder Paris }

Parisbilder

Last evening in Paris
(To the memory of Izzedin Qalaq)

At the door of his room he said
They kill us without reasons.
Do you like French wine, and les femmes distraites?
He searched the corners quickly,
But would not go through the doorway
For they could be in the closet, waiting.
We went back to the staircase. One o'clock.
Paris all asleep. Night begins from here.
From a wide boulevard on which you walk alone.
From trees you cannot see. From a body that desires.
From a bullet that will find you.
You read Kafka just to find your darkness.
Yes, I remember, it was beautiful long ago,
And Damascus was the dream's edge. I went to the river,
Which I thought to be a woman, cloistered or imprisoned.
They never let me see the river once again.
Our prisons fill the earth,
So can you still distinguish
The features on the face?
Paris sleeps in Sunday paintings waiting by the Seine
And all the city stories strangle in the smog.
Only lovers think that water can be mirrors
When they kill themselves.

Where shall we sleep?
On a bench in any park.
Might they kill us there?
They might, but I'm tired,
And I hurt from these vague stars.

As if a youth were stone
To bear the missing of his home of orange blossom
For so long,
A land for tourists
And for military monks.

He collects posters. He writes on the remains
Of cigarettes his views of his oppressors.
They find a village, they destroy it,
Then they rest upon the grass.
They admit they murdered me,
Then they take me in their arms.

They told me that they'd give me
Twenty thousand francs
For a speech in which I would convince
The French gauchistes that the prisons on the West Bank
Were really only clinics,
That my wounds were really only roses.

He let himself be trailed by the eyes
That knew his shadow. Crowded by the streets,
By the friends on their way to solitary confinement
Or to the latest film.
Crowded by a night so full of night,
And of rotten language.
He would say his last goodbye to me
Every time we met
Since in his mind he pictured me
Following his coffin. Rising from the flowers,
He could ask:
Are you now convinced
That they kill us without reasons?

He would fall in love, and then forget.

But he remembered every leaf on every plant
That grew alongside roads
That led from Northern Palestine.

The songs that bid the refugee farewell,
The songs that bid the conqueror to stay
Resemble one another.

Have you thought of suicide,
Like all your generation?
Like all my generation,
I loved a girl of sea.
The evening would lie bleeding at her window
For no wound. I stood and called:
The echo came back stone.
Why am I not of copper
To bear the weight of this?

Do you remember childhood,
How we snatched our hearts and fingers
From the brown cats that lived outside the door.
We went to shore and called:
The echo came back moon.

At the old jail in Haifa
I learned how women could be countries.

My friend was jumping now,
Like a bird wet with years of thunder.
My mother loves Damascus. My father wishes he could sleep
On the stones that sleep inside his soul. My sister
Thinks the Gulf is far away. She thinks my blood
Can break a sword. She thinks my blood can break the rules.
I am a native of the Carmel,
A mountain which the evening melts down into kisses.
I lay under the pines for fifteen winters.
The rain drenched me, so I sought the hermit priest.
He prayed before me and he prayed for me.
The mountain spread in me like body hair.

And did you sing to her?

Call her what you will.
A woman, a language, a homeland, a mirror,
The unity of birds in wheatfields,
The first wave made lonely on the shore.

We sang together of the vagueness that enwrapped us.

In the passage you sleep alone in your own arms alone
Your lovers have all neared their daggers in the small
passage you sleep alone the sea touches your affections
The sea breaks you the sea breaks your lovers have all left
their swords the earth is smaller than your silence
Your body smaller than a knifestab in the small passage
You sleep alone between yourself and I between myself
and you alone in your arms alone

Is a man like us allowed to ponder painting
Or the origin of God?
Can he say he knows the way a sparrow's wing
Resembles his mother's wave farewell?
Can he walk in St. Germain,
Or see the tour like any tourist?

I have not found the woman yet
The woman who might touch my hair
And make the evening loiter on the bridges.

He knows that soldiers will return.
He knows that weeds will only sprout again.
And yet he crosses all the rivers just to cross them.

In June, all Paris will head South.
Perhaps the ones who kill might also head South.
He sees his death in the wine, and asks the waiter
If he'll change his glass.
They trailed me at the poster exhibition,
So I turned around and cornered them
When I shook their hands.

He fingers death,
He knows its several kinds:
A bomb beneath the car,
And your arms and legs fly off
To break the vases that they land on
In the houses on the street.

A bomb beneath the table,
A slit beneath the throat,
A bullet in the back,
These are death,
Much simpler than you think.
It hurts only if you are afraid,
Only if you watch it coming,
Only if you watch it slowly coming.

Outside his door,
The chestnut trees
And a curve of pigeons,
At a table in the small cafe
He sees a student that he knows.
He waves, and starts up on the staircase
That leads up to his life.
He inspects his papers,
And the homeland waiting in the map.
He counts the pictures of the dead
That line his walls.
He finds the letter that his mother wrote him,
The bullet that has found him finds him
'Come home with the summer, please, my son.'

Another year only

My friends,
Those yet left alive among you
Will let me live another year
Another year only
To love a thousand women
And a thousand cities.

One year is time enough
For a thought to wear a daisy's petals,
For a girl to take me towards any sea,
For her knees to give me
Keys to all the places.
One year is time enough
To live my one great surge
My one embrace
To end the riddles of these merging times.

My friends,
Don't die as often as you have been dying,
Don't die,
Wait a year for me,
A year, another year only.
Perhaps we could finish
The many talks we started,
Perhaps we could just wander
Away from clocks and banners.
Had we spoken treason
When we named each bird a country

And each country,
Other than our wound,
A maze?
Perhaps we could guard language
From a slant we did not wish for,
From a chant we could not chant
To the priests.

My friends,
You who crowd around my bed,
Who follow me as I approach
A girl whose waist I have not touched,
Leave me be awhile.
Go away, my friends.

We have the right to taste a coffee
Touched with sweetness, not with blood.
We have the right to listen to the voices
In our fingers calling softly to the passing swallows,
Not to the dying horses.
The right to count our veins,
To thank the secret down
That waits upon our lover's skin,
To break the whining of all pious songs.

My friends,
Don't die before you ask forgiveness
Of a rose you did not see,
Of a town you did not stop in,
Of a woman free of minarets and icons.
Don't die before you ask
What the living never learn
Why the earth sometimes resembles
Quince on childhood's trees

Why did they know me clearly
When I died
Why did they all forsake me
When I came back still alive?

My friends, my familiar heroes,
Think of me a little,
Love me just a little,
Don't die as often as you have been dying
Don't die,
Wait for me a year,
Another year,
Love me so we drink this cup together,
So we see that white waves
Are not always women.
What will I do after you,
What will I do after the last burial?

How do I still love earth
That robs you from me
That hides you from the sea
How do I still love oceans
That drowned those who were praying
But left the steeples standing
Higher than before.
Where will I spend my Sunday evenings,
Who will I sit with as I watch a newborn kitten
Who will describe this lemon moon to me?
Who will hear me detail
The passing women of my daydreams

What will my life mean
When my shadow leans against me
After you?
Don't die,
Don't die as you have been dying.
Don't take me from the femaleness of fruit
To the addictive rites of mourning.

My heart is not my own
That I might throw it to you as a token.
My body is not my own
That I might let it be your coffin
Have mercy, my cruel friends,
Take pity on those who look for vistas
In the shrapnel,
On those who wait to enter blossom
Through a gate of bitter ash.
Don't disappear like this,
For who will then pick roses
For the older dead?
Should we not have some other task
Than digging graves
And seeking new words for a eulogy
To make it seem unlike the one
That we'd just written?
How small these flowers are
How deep is all this blood.

My friends,
Those yet left alive among you
Will let me live another year,
A year to walk together,
To fling a river on our backs
Like gypsies,
To break the remnants of the structure down
To bring our tired soul away from its long exile.

For if you leave me now,
If you go to live within the skull's shape,
I will not call or mourn you
Nor will I write the smallest word of sorrow
Because I can no longer mourn
This country in a body
This body in a bullet.
Let this be the end of crying
The ready elegy for all of you,
My parting friends.

Don't die, don't die
No flower is as precious in this desert
As your blood
Don't die, wait a year for me
That I might dare to go and say
To my grieving mother:
Bear me once again
That I might love love from its beginnings.
Another year only,
Another year,
Another year.

Pigeons settle, pigeons fly

Prepare the earth for me
That I might rest
As love invades me like my tiredness
Your morning is a fruit's song,
Your evening, gold.
You are the air denuding itself
Like the tears of vines
You are my soul's beginning
And its end.

I and my love are two voices
In one poem.
I am my love's own,
And he is the distant star's.
We enter a dream that slows itself
Until we cannot find it.
When my love sleeps
I wake to guard his dream from what he sees,
I wake to brush away those nights
That passed before we met.
I pick our days by hand
As he picked the table's roses.
Sleep, my love,
That the sea might reach my knees,
Sleep, my love,
I give you my two braids,
I give you peace.

I saw April on the sea
And said
I have forgotten your hands' attention.
How many times can you be born in dreams,
How many times can I be killed by you?
I call you before language
I fly to your waist before I reach you.
You place in the beaks of pigeons
The addresses of my soul
And disappear like the distance
In the fields
Until I find
You are the whole of Egypt,
You are Babel and Damascus.

Where are you taking me to, my love,
So far from my father's house,
From my narrow bed and boredom,
From my mirrors, from my moon,
From my sleeplessness and girlhood.
You let the high waves carry me away.
Because I love you
My waist bleeds
I run in pain through nights
Made wider by my fear
I love for I desire.
I love for I desire.
I hold this ray of light
Covered with bright bees

I fear for my heart from you
I fear that I might reach
What I desire
I tame my spirit till it takes your shape.
I rub my wounds against your silence's edge
I die, that speech might wait upon you.

Pigeons settle, pigeons fly.

Because I love you
Water cuts me
The roads to the ocean wound me
Butterflies hurt me
I call you and I fear your awareness,
Because I love you
The shadows beneath a streetlight hurt me
A bird in the far sky hurts me
The smell of violets
The sea's beginning
I wish I did not love
That this marble might yet heal.

Pigeons settle, pigeons fly.

I see you and escape dying.
Your body is a shore
Of ten white lilies
Ten buds that give the sky
The blue that it had lost

I touch this marble
I worship your shore of early spring,
Of salt and ancient honey
I drink the nectar of your night
And sleep on wheat that breaks the field,
That breaks the echo so it rusts.
My love
I fear the silence of your hands
So rub my blood
That these stallions might grow calm
My love
The female birds fly to you
So take me as your spirit
Or your spouse
My love
I'll stay with you with you with you
Because you are my sky's roof
And my body is your earth upon this earth.

Pigeons settle, pigeons fly.

I saw on the bridge
The Andalusia of love
And the sixth sense
He gave her back her heart
And said
Your love has cost me
What I do not love
Your love has cost me
The moon slept
On a broken ring
On the ring they broke
And the birds flew away.

I saw on the bridge
Andalusian love and the sixth sense.
She gave him back his heart
And said
Your love has cost me
What I will not pay
Your love has cost me
The moon slept on a broken ring
The birds flew away
Or came to roost
On the bridge
Made dark by lovers parting.

Index of first lines

A clear street 17
A man and a woman parting 31
At night 29
At the door of his room 61
Butterfly of stone 49
Earth narrows before us 5
Endless place of thought 9
I asked you to take me 33
I love the seas I love 43
If I could choose again from the beginning 1
My friends 67
On Fifth Avenue he greeted me 35
Prepare the earth for me 73
The flute speaks 7
The Nile has its habits 11
The river is the stranger 25
They arrive 19
We know place 59
We walk towards a land 2
We will meet in a while 45
When my words were wheat 41
Woman who holds the Mediterranean 47